Probabilistic Data Structures

Aditya Chatterjee

Ethan Z. Booker

Content

Preface

This book "**Probabilistic Data Structures**" is an Introduction to Probabilistic Data Structures and aims to introduce the readers to ideas of randomness in Data Structure design.

It is easier to understand randomness in algorithms with examples such as randomly splitting array in Quick Sort but most programmers fail to realize that Data Structures can be probabilistic as well.

In this, not only the answer is probabilistic but also the structure.

In fact, **Google's Chrome browser** uses a Probabilistic Data Structure within it. Read on to find out which data structure it is and how it is used.

The ideas have been presented in a simple language (avoiding technical terms) with intuitive insights which will help anyone to go through this book and enjoy the knowledge.

This knowledge will help you to design better systems suited for real use.

Authors: Aditya Chatterjee, Ethan Z. Booker

Aditya is a Founding member at OpenGenus; Ethan has been an Intern at OpenGenus and a student at University of Wisconsin, La Crosse;

First Edition: January 2021

Introduction to Probabilistic Data Structures

When it comes to answers we often want the precise exact answer, but there comes a time and place where getting the exact answer may take up significant resources and we would be fine with an approximate answer that is close to the correct answer.

Take for instance, Big Data; As Big Data deals with massive amounts of data and processing time, often times the standard data structures such as a hash map, hash set are just not feasible for the problems that are encountered. Big Data problems tend to deal with running out of memory or deterministic data structures taking too long to process.

These issues brought rise for a new type of data structures that gives us an approximately good enough answer which is known as using a probabilistic data structure.

Probabilistic Data Structure

By using this type of data structure, we can only safely assume that we have an approximate solution which may or may not be the exact answer, but it is in the right direction. These data structures are proven to use either a fixed or sublinear memory and have constant execution time. As mentioned before, the answers may not be exact and have some probability of error.

Any probabilistic data structure will rely on some form of probability such as using randomness, hashing, and others to reach an approximate solution.

Some of the data structures are rather proven alternative approaches for a data structure but often they are needed for these cases:

- analyzing / mining big data sets (more than what a deterministic data structure can handle).
- Statistical analysis
- A stream of data that need an answer

List of Probabilistic Data Structures

Here is a list of data structures that we have organized in a manner of which their purpose is used for. A small description about each data structure is included.

Frequency

- Count-min Sketch

Memory efficient hash table approach using 1 or more hash functions to estimate (overestimation) frequency counts.

Ranking

- Random Sampling

Uses an internal random selecting algorithm to perform quick linear time random selecting. Useful if you need only a sublist of options without any prioritization.

- q-digest

This data structure is complete binary tree over a set of values where it keeps track of frequency and propagates an estimate of the lower frequency values. Originally was designed for sensor networks but found a place in rank-based statistics.

- t-digest

Useful for detecting anomalies and is typically a tree-based data structure that handles a stream of integers to handle such queries like quantiles, percentiles, and other rank-based statistics.

Similarity

- MinHash

A useful data structure for estimating similarity between two sets of data (strings, numbers, etc) using Jaccard similarity metrics and uses one or more hash functions to quickly evaluate.

- SimHash

Like the idea of MinHash but relies on the items to have a hash function along with comparing the corresponding bits by using some metric like the hamming distance.

Cardinality

- LogLog

An algorithm that can be structured into a data structure that deals with distinct elements in a set. It's very quick and can handle lots of elements with less memory than a normal set.

- HyperLogLog

An extension of the LogLog which uses a different way of measuring the distinct difference count.

Membership

- Bloom Filter

A data structure that mimics a hash table but uses bytes from a hash code to determine position and if that element exists. It uses less memory and approximates if an element exists in a set.

- Counting Bloom filter

Simply a generalized version of the bloom filter which allows a threshold count number to query the set.

- Quotient Filter

A modified version of bloom filter which includes metadata about the buckets. This uses more memory than the bloom filter but less than the counting bloom filter.

- Cuckoo Filter

Perhaps a more compact version of the bloom filter while allowing the delete operation to be implementable. This uses the cuckoo hashing approach.

Not Classified

- Hash Tables
- Kinetic Hanger

A heap where inserts and deletes don't need to balance and can be randomized while still maintaining competitive heap performance.

- Kinetic Heater

A prioritized queue similar to the kinetic hanger but in practice not as efficient as the better kinetic priority queues.

- Skip List

An ordered-key based data structure that allows for competitive performance dictionary or list while implementation remaining relatively easy. This data structure proves that probability can work along with being able to quick index certain items based on probability.

- Random Tree

Uses stochastic properties while maintain tree-like properties. This has proven to applicable uses in fractals, machine learning, and etc.

Notes

It's important to know that each data structure have their own niche purposes, but some can be used for other purposes though it's up to you to decide which is data structure is appropriate to use.

All these data structures can have slight various implementation differences providing different amounts of error or performance.

Such as adding a margin of error threshold or creating deterministic-like behavior within a probabilistic data structure.

Just like how there are probabilistic data structures, there are probabilistic algorithms that also give an approximate solution.

Probabilistic Algorithms and Link with Data Structures

Randomness in algorithms is common.

Some examples of Probabilistic Algorithms are:

- **Randomly selecting Pivot in Quick Sort**

In Quick Sort, pivot is an element which is used to split the array into two components. Calculations show that randomly choosing a pivot gives equally good performance than deterministic methods like median of medians.

- **Random searching and sorting**

Such algorithms are common and easy to understand but is not used. This is because the real Probabilistic Algorithms include some more insights to improve over the deterministic counterpart.

- **Hash Map**

Many fail to realize that Hash Map is a probabilistic data structure/ algorithmic technique. Though in this case, we can eliminate the probabilistic nature by collision resolution (that is handling collisions).

This comes from the fact that multiple elements can be hashed to the same value and if we do not handle collision, we keep losing track of the original element and hence, this leads to some error.

This idea will form the basis of several Probabilistic Data Structures.

Generating a random number is fundamental in this (note: this is not needed for every data structure or algorithm; see the case of hash map).

In terms of algorithms, random numbers can be of the following types:

- **Physical randomness**: Randomness from nature whose laws are difficult to predict.
- **Cryptographically secure pseudo randomness**: A sequence of random elements based on a Physical random element.
- **Statistical pseudo randomness**: Random elements that pass some basic statistical tests.

In terms of use, there are 2 types of Probabilistic Algorithms:

- **Las Vegas**: Fails with a probability; We can identify when it failed.
- **Monte Carlo**: Fails with a probability; We **cannot** identify when it failed.

Similar is the classification of Probabilistic Data Structures. Mainly, there are two major types:

- **Type 1**: Answer generated is right or wrong bounded by a given probability; Often, we can tell when the answer is either right or wrong.
- **Type 2**: Answer generated is always correct; The structure of the Data Structure depends on randomness.

Basic Probabilistic Data Structures

There are two basic probabilistic Data Structures:

- Hash Map without collision resolution
- Random Binary Tree

Hash Map is a fundamentally strong Data Structure that allows us to search a dataset of any size in constant time (that is instantly). This comes at the cost of large memory (usually much larger than the actual dataset).

The basic idea is to map different elements to different integer representation and use this as the index to store the original element or some information related to the element.

Apart from the memory overhead, two distinct elements can be hashed to the same value. If we do not handle this case, we fail to identify which element was the original element.

Consider: 5 and 6 are hashed to 2. If we are given 2, we cannot say if it was 5 or 6.

This can be handled by collision resolution techniques where the common one is to use a Linked List for each hash value to store multiple elements. This makes Hash Map linear in worst case but it works in constant time in practice.

As we move on, we will see how this core idea is evolved into several different and effective Probabilistic Data Structures.

Random Binary Tree

A Binary Tree is useful only if it is balanced.

This is because if un-balanced, in the worst case, Binary Tree will be same as an array.

For this, we have several self-balancing Binary Trees such as AA Trees and AVL trees. This balancing operation is an overhead which we can avoid but keeping the structure of Binary Tree random.

If we keep the Binary Tree structure random, then it may not be perfectly balanced but on average, calculations show that it is very close to a Balanced Binary Tree and delivers good performance.

A random Binary Tree is different from a Random Hash Map in the sense, that a random Binary Tree always results in the right answer and is random only from the point of its structure.

As we move on, we will come across a modified Probabilistic version of Random Binary Tree as well.

Read on. The next 5 Probabilistic Data Structures are the ones that is currently used in practice and is rich in knowledge.

Count Min Sketch

A count min sketch data structure is a probabilistic data structure that keeps track of frequency. In other words, the data structure keeps track of how many times a specific object has appeared.

Why use it?

The most common solution to the problem of keeping track of frequency is using a hash map.

 In Hash map, we keep set of elements **{element, frequency of element}**.

If element E is not in hash map, then E is inserted as {E, 1}.

If element E is already present in the hash map as {E, F} (F is the frequency of E till the previous element), then the entry is updated as {E, F+1}.

With this, we can get the frequency of all elements in O(N) time complexity which is reasonable as we need to traverse all N elements at least once.

However, there are two main issues using a hash map for this problem:

- Collision issue
- Memory overhead

Collision issue

Often a hash map will have to dynamically grow its number of buckets/ internal storage to hold all the data.

This means that there is a chance for a collision to happen as the hash function can map multiple elements to the same value. This would mean equality checks would be needed to find the key. Thus, the performance is slower.

Memory issue

Another issue is that a hash map can be memory intensive and could be a problem if you want to not use too much memory. When you have over a million unique objects then that could become quite memory intensive as keeping a reference takes requires memory along with the contents within the object itself takes memory.

So how does count min sketch solve the problems of a hash map?

A count min sketch data structure is an alternative approach that can save memory while keeping high performance at the cost of accuracy. By accuracy, we mean that the answer we will get may not be the actual answer but will be within a certain percentage close to the real answer.

Index ->	0	1	2	3	4	5	6	7	8	9	10	11	12	13	14	15
Hash function 1 ->	0	1	0	0	0	0	0	0	0	0	0	0	0	0	0	0
Hash function 2 ->	0	0	0	0	0	0	1	0	0	0	0	0	0	0	0	0
Hash function 3 ->	0	0	0	1	0	0	0	0	0	0	0	0	0	0	0	0
Hash function 4 ->	0	1	0	0	0	0	0	0	0	0	0	0	0	0	0	0

This image shows a representation of what the data structure tries to do, which is creating rows of width (w) number of buckets along an associated hash function for each row.

The number of rows is determined by the number of hash functions, so technically yes you could only have 1 hash function but the more you have the more likely you will be more accurate (if the buckets are reasonable).

The width of each row (number of buckets) is up to the testing. There is no magic number but you can guarantee good results if there are more buckets than possible values but that defeats the purpose of saving memory, so you should aim for a number less than the total number of values through testing different widths.

A count min sketch uses the idea of a hash function and buckets to keep count but uses multiple hash functions and rows of buckets to figure out the count. Using a count min sketch will always result in an **overestimate of the true count**, so you will never get an underestimate of the true count.

For example: a number may have only appeared 5 times but due to collisions it may be 10 times. Or perhaps a number never appeared but will have a count greater than 0 due to the hash values corresponding to a bucket with a positive count value.

The idea behind this is that even if a collision happens, there are other rows to check and hope that there were not many collisions either. With enough buckets and enough high quality hash functions then an exact value could potentially be found but there is a chance for an overestimate.

The count min sketch does not need to store a reference of the object nor keep the object around for later, it only needs to compute the hash value as the column index and update the count for that hash function row.

What's important to take note is that the more **high-quality hash functions** you have and sufficient enough buckets, then the better the accuracy will be. However, you also to play around with the number of buckets, too little buckets will cause collisions but too many buckets will cause a waste of space.

Now that you the fundamental idea behind this data structure, it is important to know the standard functions that come with this data structure.

Functions

The two major functionalities that a count min sketch implement are:

- put/ update
- get/ estimate

The two functions can have different names, but these are the common names that appear in different code implementations. The follow functions are written in java.

These two functions should be included in the implementation section to be fully functional.

Put / Update

```java
public void update(T item, int count)
{
    for (int row = 0; row < depth; row++)
    {
        frequencyMatrix[row]
            [boundHashCode(hashers[row].hash(item))]
+= count;
```

```
            }
    }
```

The code fragment above is a method that takes the item that you want
to give an associated count to. A count min data structure typically has
multiple rows, so you would iterate through each row and use the hash
function to find which bucket the count will be added to. There is a
possibility that the hash function creates a value that is greater than the
length of the row, so the hash code is bounded to the value of 0 to row
length - 1.

Get / Estimate

```
public int estimate(T item) {
    int count = Integer.MAX_VALUE;
        for (int row = 0; row < depth; row++) {
        count = Math.min(count,
frequencyMatrix[row][boundHashCode(hashers[row].hash(i
tem))]);
        }
    return count;
}
```

Now because this is probabilistic and there is a chance for collision, we
have to go through each row and find the corresponding bucket index
that item would appear in and find the minimum amount.

The reason why we want the minimum is because we can guarantee the
position where it should be but not the value if there are collisions on a
few rows. As the implementation of add will simply handle collisions by
adding onto the current value at that bucket position, it's safe to check
the other rows as it's extremely unlikely for two objects of different

values to have the same hash values (assuming it's a good hash function) for each row.

Implementation

The following is a possible implementation of how a count min sketch in Java.

```java
import java.util.HashMap;
import java.util.Random;

public class CountMinSketch<T>
{
        public static interface Hasher<T>
        {
                public int hash(T obj);
        }

        private int depth;
        private int width;
        private Hasher<T>[] hashers;
        private int[][] frequencyMatrix;

        @SafeVarargs
        public CountMinSketch(int width, Hasher<T>...
hashers)
        {
                this.width = width;
                this.hashers = hashers;
                depth = hashers.length;
                frequencyMatrix = new int[depth][width];
        }

        public void update(T item, int count)
        {
```

```java
                //implementation was shown in the
section above
                for (int row = 0; row < depth; row++)
                {
                frequencyMatrix[row]
                [boundHashCode(hashers[row].hash(item))]
+= count;
                }
        }

        public int estimate(T item)
        {
                //implementation was shown in the
section above
                int count = Integer.MAX_VALUE;
                for (int row = 0; row < depth; row++) {
                count = Math.min(count,
frequencyMatrix[row][boundHashCode(hashers[row].hash(i
tem))]);
                }
                return count;

        }

    //Keep the hash code within 0 and length of row -
1.
        private int boundHashCode(int hashCode)
        {
                return hashCode % width;
        }

        public static void main(String[] args)
        {
                //Using functional programming to create
these.
                CountMinSketch.Hasher<Integer> hasher1 =
number -> number;
                CountMinSketch.Hasher<Integer> hasher2 =
number -> {
```

```java
                    String strForm =
String.valueOf(number);
                    int hashVal = 0;
                    for (int i = 0; i <
strForm.length(); i++) {
                        hashVal =
strForm.charAt(i) + (31 * hashVal);
                    }
                    return hashVal;
                };
                CountMinSketch.Hasher<Integer> hasher3 =
number -> {
                    number ^= (number << 13);
                    number ^= (number >> 17);
                    number ^= (number << 5);
                    return Math.abs(number);
                };

                CountMinSketch.Hasher<Integer> hasher4 =
number -> String.valueOf(number).hashCode();

        int numberOfBuckets = 16;
                CountMinSketch<Integer> cms = new
CountMinSketch<>(numberOfBuckets, hasher1, hasher2,
hasher3, hasher4);
                Random rand = new Random();
        //Using a hashmap to keep track of the real
count
                HashMap<Integer, Integer> freqCount =
new HashMap<>();
                int maxIncrement = 10;
                int maxNumber = 1000;
                int iterations = 50;
        //add 50 random numbers with a count of 1-10
                for (int i = 0; i < iterations; i++) {
                    int increment =
rand.nextInt(maxIncrement) + 1;
                    int number =
rand.nextInt(maxNumber);
```

```
                    freqCount.compute(number, (k, v)
-> v == null ? increment : v + increment);
                    cms.update(number, increment);
            }

        //Print out all the numbers that were added
with their real and estimated count.
                for (Integer key : freqCount.keySet()) {
                    System.out.println("For key: " +
key + "\t real count: " + freqCount.get(key) + "\t
estimated count: "

                                        +

cms.estimate(key));
                }
        }
}
```

Some important things in the above implementation to take note:

- The update and estimate function implementations are in the sections above.
- We have created a generic hasher interface and count min sketch data structure to allow flexibility in what values to hash. Though if you were working with strings or some primitive data type then you could simply change the types to suit what you want.
- Inside the main function we have created 4 hash functions that deal with integers (they are not the best hash functions but can work) using functional programming.
- Try to play around with the number of buckets, iterations, increment amount, and max number to get a better observation of the effects.
- Also try removing a few of the hash functions and you will notice that the accuracy will decrease with less rows.

Pros and Cons

Pros

- Very simple and easy to implement.
- Can minimize memory greatly and avoid equality checks.
- Customizable data structure to provide your own hash functions and the number of buckets.
- Can guarantee the value will be either be exact or an overestimate.

Cons

- A good chance the count is not exact, will probably be overestimate.
- Such as a value never appeared once but will have a positive frequency count.
- Requires good hash functions.
- Requires testing around to get the benefits of the data structure.

Other Applications

Besides being used for an alternative method of keeping track of a relative frequency count, there are other uses this data structure may be used in.

- Possibly for a safe password picking mechanism.
- passwords that are popular could be declined.
- passwords that are extremely rare could have a high amount due to collisions which could also be declined.
- This would mean passwords may need to be varied for this application.
- In NLP (natural language processing), keeping frequency count on a large amount of data such as pairs / triplets can be reduced by using this data structure.
- Heavily useful in queries too such as avoiding going through the entire table of data and use approximate values to speed up queries.

- There are other applications such as: heavy hitters, approximate page rank, distinct count and many more.

MinHash

Let us assume you wanted to find how similar two sets are. You could simply brute force your way by going through the contents of one set and compare those elements with the other set. Sure, this method will work but what if you wanted to check a bunch of other sets? This would be rather slow, especially if you are working with a lot of data.

We will go through some basics of set first.

A set is a collection of distinct elements. This means each element in the set can only appear once.

- Invalid set: A = { 1, 1, 2, 3, 4, 4, 4, 5}, has duplicate 1's and 4's.
- Valid set: A = { 1, 2, 3, 4, 5 }, has no duplicates
- Valid set: A = { }, empty set

The intersection between two sets results in a set that contains elements both sets A and B share.

Given sets: A = { 1, 2, 3 }, B = { 3, 4, 5 }

A ∩ B = { 3 }.

The union between two sets is both sets A and B combined together and removing duplicate copies of elements.

Given sets: A = { 1, 2, 3 }, B = { 3, 4, 5 }

A ∪ B = { 1, 2, 3, 4, 5 }

The size of a set is the number of elements in a given set denoted by | set | .

Given set: A = { 1, 2, 3, 4, 5 }

| A | = 5, because there are 5 elements.

Jaccard Similarity

Some of you may know this equation and how to apply it, so you may skip this section.

$$J(A,B) = \frac{|A \cap B|}{|A \cup B|} = \frac{|A \cap B|}{|A| + |B| - |A \cap B|}$$

For those that are unfamiliar with Jaccard similarity, then this will be important.

The image above shows the equation of how to calculate the Jaccard similarity which is a numeric score to compare similarity between two sets.

The equation states that you need to calculate the size of the intersection between A and B then divide by the size of the union of A and B.

This equation can be translated into the size of the intersection between A and B divided by size of A plus size of B minus the intersection between A and B.

Using the information above, you could work out simple sets to determine the Jaccard similarity number.

The problem stated at the beginning of the chapter briefly covered the idea of finding Jaccard similarity but rather in an obscure way, but nonetheless trying to find the exact value is too time consuming.

MinHash Data Structure solves this problem.

MinHash

MinHash was originally an algorithm to **quickly estimate the Jaccard similarity** between two sets but can be designed as a data structure that revolves around the algorithm. This is a **probabilistic data structure that quickly estimates how similar two sets are**.

The idea behind MinHash is representing each set as a signature. A signature preserves a permutation of a bit array representation of a set. By using hash functions that simulate a permutation, the probability of collisions against all permutations results to the Jaccard similarity.

This is hard to grasp, so I will walk you through what is happening.

Probabilistic Nature

The probabilistic nature behind this data structure is purely through the hash functions in the signature matrix. You will get a better understanding when you walk through the steps, but for now bear with me. This has functions in the signature matrix that determine the performance of the data structure.

Not having enough hash functions will cause small number of comparisons to properly gauge similarity between two sets due to all the values probably colliding. However, it is essential to create/ use **high quality distributed hash algorithms** (could look them up) as it is unlikely to have a similar value during similarity comparison time. The more high-quality hash functions you have, the better the evaluation of similarity will result, but there is a threshold, so you must test your results and see.

Regardless, a hash function is the pivotal part needed but there are not enough out there as you may want a lot. If you need more hash functions, then you could:

- use 1 hash function and go through the process of salting, which is basically rehashing a hash code over and over or
- you could create your own way to manipulate the hash code through proper bit manipulation, but salting is a very easy and efficient solution. These salted hash codes would still result be good enough to act as a hash function that hashed those values.

Despite having quick performance, since hash functions are limited to a certain range of values and collisions are bound to happen, the similarity is not always accurate.

What the process looks like?

So what exactly does the MinHash data structure do? Well it is an algorithm but can be converted into a data structure and we will explain the process of creating it.

Input matrix

	S₁	S₂	S₃	S₄
A	1	0	1	0
B	1	0	0	1
C	0	1	0	1
D	0	1	0	1
E	0	1	0	1
F	1	0	1	0
G	1	0	1	0

≈

Signature matrix

	S₁	S₂	S₃	S₄
h₁	1	2	1	2
h₂	2	1	3	1
h₃	3	1	3	1

- Sig(S) = vector of hash values
  - e.g., $Sig(S_2) = [2,1,1]$
- Sig(S,i) = value of the i-th hash function for set S
  - E.g., $Sig(S_2,3) = 1$

Above is the picture of the steps needed for the data structure to work. If you get confused, I will explain more in-depth the following sections.

- Get a collection of sets then create an input matrix known which are just rows of bit arrays.
- This bit arrays will be the length of the universal set size (the total number of unique values).
- Create a signature matrix filled with max value.
- Iterate through the input matrix and whenever you see a non-zero value, find the corresponding set it bit belongs to and pass index value through the set of hash functions in the signature matrix and take the minimum value.

Step 1) Building each bit array representation.

The initial step is to build a bit array for each set;

However we need to know how big to make it. To do so, you need to know the universal set size which is the size of the union of all sets that will be used later to compare.

Let us assume we have 3 sets

- A = { 1, 3, 5, 7 }
- B = { 0, 2, 8, 10 }
- C = { 4, 5, 6, 8, 9, 10 }

Universal Set (A ∪ B ∪ C) = { 0, 1, 2, 3, 4, 5, 6, 7, 8, 9, 10 }

Since the size of the universal set is 11, we will make each bit array size 11. Then you will go through each element in a set and get the hash code then bound that hash code with the total size of the universal set. Once you find the bounded hash code, you will represent that element as present denoting it as a value that is not 0, such as 1.

In this case, let us assume the hash code of a number is the number itself. This would result in bit arrays:

- Bit array A = [0, 1, 0, 1, 0, 1, 0, 1, 0, 0, 0]
- Bit array B = [1, 0, 1, 0, 0, 0, 0, 0, 1, 0, 1]
- Bit array C = [0, 0, 0, 0, 1, 1, 1, 0, 1, 1, 1]

Universal Set Size

```
private int getUniversalSetSize(Set<T>... sets)
{
        Set<T> universalSet = new HashSet<>();
        for (Set<T> set : sets)
        {
                universalSet.addAll(set);
        }
        return universalSet.size();
```

```
}
```

The code above is an example of how one might find the universal size of all sets put together.

Building Bit Arrays

```
private int[][] buildBinaryDocSet(Set<T>... sets)
{
        int[][] binaryDocSet = new
int[sets.length][totalFeatures()];

        for (int setIdx = 0; setIdx < sets.length;
setIdx++)
        {
                for (T feature : sets[setIdx])
                {
        binaryDocSet[setIdx][bound(feature.hashCode())]
= 1;
                }
        }

        return binaryDocSet;
}
```

We are simply iterating through each set and updating the bit array to represent our set.

- totalFeatures() is the universal set size.
- bound(hashcode) is simply hashcode % universal set size
- Step 2 Building the Signature Matrix

- After building the bit array representations, this is where minhash matrix is built.
- Rows of the matrix are denoted by a hash function.
- Columns of the matrix are denoted by the sets' indices.

```java
private int[][] buildSignatureMatrix()
{
        int[][] sigMatrix = initSigMatrix();

        for (int feature = 0; feature <
totalFeatures(); feature++)
        {
                for (int document = 0; document <
totalDocuments(); document++)
                {
                        if
(binaryDocSet[document][feature] != 0)
                        {

        computeSigHashes(sigMatrix, document, feature);
                        }
                }
        }

        return sigMatrix;
}
```

To clarify:

- feature and features refers to elements of a set
- document refers to a specific index of a set.

The idea behind this method is to go through each bit array and whenever we see a non-zero value, we will update our signature matrix calling computeSigHashes function.

It is important to initialize the matrix with all maximum values because we will be calling Math.min function to preserve the property of a signature matrix.

```
private void computeSigHashes(int[][] sigMatrix, int
document, int feature)
{
      for (int hasher = 0; hasher <
totalHashFunctions(); hasher++)
        {
            sigMatrix[hasher][document] =
Math.min(sigMatrix[hasher][document],
bound(hashers[hasher].hash(feature)));
        }
}
```

Go through each hash function and the associated set index and then select the minimum value between the current value in the signature matrix and the bounded hashed index.

Similarities

After building the signature table, calculating an estimate of the Jaccard similarty will be easy.

```
public double similarity(int docIndex1, int docIndex2)
{
      int similar = 0;
      for (int hasher = 0; hasher <
totalHashFunctions(); hasher++)
```

```
        {
            if (signatureMatrix[hasher][docIndex1]
== signatureMatrix[hasher][docIndex2])
            {
                similar++;
            }
        }

        return (double) similar / totalHashFunctions();
}
```

Go down each row of the matrix and compare the set index for both. If they have the same value, increment a running count.

Lastly, divide the running count by the total rows (aka total number of hash functions).

Code

Here is the full code of all the segments, I have renamed some of the terms because originally this algorithm was developed for web searches but has since then found other applications.

```
import java.util.Arrays;
import java.util.HashSet;
import java.util.Set;

public class MinHash<T> {
        public interface Hasher {
                int hash(int item);
        }

        private int totalFeatures;
        private int[][] binaryDocSet;
        private int[][] signatureMatrix;
        private Hasher[] hashers;
```

```java
        @SafeVarargs
        public MinHash(Hasher[] hashers, Set<T>... sets) {
                this.hashers = hashers;
                totalFeatures = getUniversalSetSize(sets);
                binaryDocSet = buildBinaryDocSet(sets);
                signatureMatrix = buildSignatureMatrix();
        }

        @SafeVarargs
        private int getUniversalSetSize(Set<T>... sets) {
                Set<T> universalSet = new HashSet<>();
                for (Set<T> set : sets) {
                        universalSet.addAll(set);
                }
                return universalSet.size();
        }

        //Better to store in a sparse matrix
        @SafeVarargs
        private int[][] buildBinaryDocSet(Set<T>... sets) {
                int[][] binaryDocSet = new
int[sets.length][totalFeatures()];

                for (int setIdx = 0; setIdx < sets.length;
setIdx++) {
                        for (T feature : sets[setIdx]) {

        binaryDocSet[setIdx][bound(feature.hashCode())] =
1;
                        }
                }

                return binaryDocSet;
        }

        private int[][] buildSignatureMatrix() {
                int[][] sigMatrix = initSigMatrix();

                for (int feature = 0; feature <
totalFeatures(); feature++) {
                        for (int document = 0; document <
totalDocuments(); document++) {
```

```java
                            if
(binaryDocSet[document][feature] != 0) {

            computeSigHashes(sigMatrix, document, feature);
                            }
                    }
            }

            return sigMatrix;
        }

        private int[][] initSigMatrix() {
                int[][] sigMatrix = new
int[totalHashFunctions()][totalDocuments()];
                for (int[] vector : sigMatrix) {
                        Arrays.fill(vector,
Integer.MAX_VALUE);
                }
                return sigMatrix;
        }

        private void computeSigHashes(int[][] sigMatrix,
int document, int feature) {
                for (int hasher = 0; hasher <
totalHashFunctions(); hasher++) {
                        sigMatrix[hasher][document] =
Math.min(sigMatrix[hasher][document],
bound(hashers[hasher].hash(feature)));
                }
        }

        public double similarity(int docIndex1, int
docIndex2) {
                int similar = 0;
                for (int hasher = 0; hasher <
totalHashFunctions(); hasher++) {
                        if
(signatureMatrix[hasher][docIndex1] ==
signatureMatrix[hasher][docIndex2]) {
                                similar++;
                }
            }
```

```java
                    return (double) similar /
totalHashFunctions();
        }

        private int bound(int hash) {
                return hash % totalFeatures();
        }

        public int totalFeatures() {
                return totalFeatures;
        }

        public int totalDocuments() {
                return binaryDocSet.length;
        }

        public int totalHashFunctions() {
                return hashers.length;
        }

        public static void main(String[] arsgs) {
                Hasher h1 = num -> (22 * num + 5) % 31;
                Hasher h2 = num -> (30 * num + 2) % 31;
                Hasher h3 = num -> (21 * num + 23) % 31;
                Hasher h4 = num -> (15 * num + 6) % 31;
                Hasher[] hashers = { h1, h2, h3, h4 };

                Set<Integer> doc1 = new
HashSet<>(Arrays.asList(8, 15, 16));
                Set<Integer> doc2 = new
HashSet<>(Arrays.asList(1, 5, 7, 10, 11, 15, 16, 17));
                Set<Integer> doc3 = new
HashSet<>(Arrays.asList(0, 1, 2, 3, 4, 5, 7, 9, 12, 17));
                Set<Integer> doc4 = new
HashSet<>(Arrays.asList(1, 5, 6, 13, 14, 15));
                Set<Integer> doc5 = new
HashSet<>(Arrays.asList(1, 2, 5, 9, 13, 15, 18));

                MinHash<Integer> minhash = new
MinHash<>(hashers, doc1, doc2, doc3, doc4, doc5);
                System.out.println(minhash.similarity(1,
2)); //doc2, doc3
                System.out.println(minhash.similarity(3,
4)); //doc4, doc5
```

```
                    System.out.println(minhash.similarity(0,
2)); //doc1, doc3
        }
}
```

This code shows you an example of sets using numbers from 0 through 18.

Pros and Cons

- The minhash similarity number is an estimate of the Jaccard similarity, so sometimes there is a margin of error.
- MinHash has many different variations such as B-bit which uses bits to save a good amount of memory rather than using purely arrays of ints while still preserving easy implementation.
- The more refined quality hash functions that you provide, the less the error of similarity will be but at the cost of more memory.
- You must define your own permutation hash functions which means you need to have an understanding of how quality hash functions are created.
- Often a prime number is involved.

Applications

- Near-duplicates detection
- Search industry, machine learning systems, content matching, and many more.

LogLog Data Structure

Imagine you had a problem where you were asked to find the **number of unique elements** in a list of data where there could be duplicates. There are 2 quick approaches one could quickly come up with.

- One option is simply to rely on the Hash Set but often they have to deal with resizing the array of hash map, deal with collisions, deal with equality checks.
- The other option would be simply to sort the list of data then simply iterate through the list and gather non-duplicates.

Both of this work fine for small amount of data but when there is a large amount of data in the data set then it becomes an unfeasible approach.

Introduction to LogLog

Illustrated in the problem section is what is known as **cardinality**, where your goal is to find the number of distinct elements in set of data where duplicates can exist.

The need for a better solution was in need due to the **large datasets in Big Data**.

Before diving into LogLog, it is best to understand the basis of how LogLog came about.

Simple Counter / FM Sketch

This is the simplest approach for cardinality where essentially:

- You have a bit map and hash the key

- Then with the hash code, you would find the first 1 bit starting left to right
- Then, update the corresponding index at that bit.

Now imagine, having more than 1 bit map as they will serve as buckets to lower the probability of error.

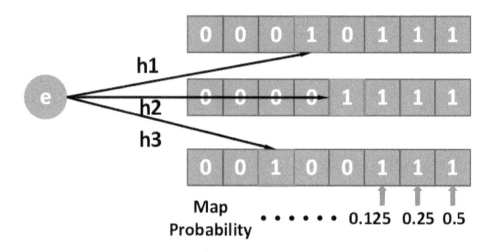

This is an example of multiple simple counters. By having more counters, we lower the error of cardinality but at the cost of an increase of memory.

LogLog

Why did I explain what a simple counter was?

Essentially, LogLog wanted to minimize the memory needed for multiple simple counters while also minimizing the high error rate that simple counters method had.

Rather than needing multiple simple counters, the LogLog approach allocates enough buckets to store the counts thus reducing the memory needed while also reducing the error rate.

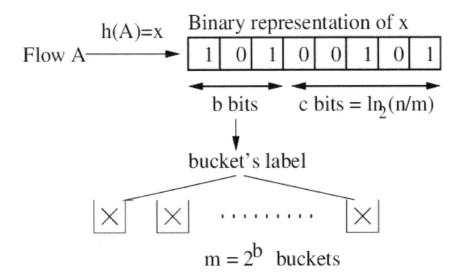

The idea is to utilize the hash code. The first X bits of the hash code is dedicated towards determining which bucket it belongs to. The bits after the first X bits are dedicated to ranking (giving it a value based on some rank algorithm).

Though not mentioned in most implementations, but 32 bit binary representation is used because it covers most values generated, but for our implementation we will use 64 as that represents a long range.

Lastly, to calculate the cardinality, you would simple sum all the values in the buckets, average that value, then apply it to a stochastic formula.

Probabilistic Nature

For most probabilistic data structures, it is heavily reliant on a hash function or another means of probability. As for this, LogLog, the hash function will heavily determine the results of cardinality.

If you are not aware, if the hash function does not properly distribute then lots of collisions will happen. These collisions are not good because this would influence which buckets get selected and what values would be inside of them. This is not what is intended.

Obviously, you should pick a good hash function.

Take for example, if you had 1024 buckets, you could estimate 10^8 with a standard error of 4% where each register had 5 bits.

Hash Function

Before implementing, you need a very good hash function. Most implementations use **Murmur3** Hash which is very good and proven hash function.

This hash function is important for the internals of this data structure, so it is important to select a high quality hash function.

Getting the Bucket Index

Simply you define how many buckets you want, often it is a power of 2. You need to determine how many bits are required to get that bucket number.

This is described in the previous picture of the LogLog, where the "b bits" represent bucket bits (the first X bits). Once you know how many bits are required, you get the binary representation of the hash code and you take the first X bits then find the integer value of those bits and make sure it is bounded within the range of 0 to totalBuckets-1.

Ranking

This is described in the picture of LogLog, where the "c bits" represent bucket bits (the bits after the first X bits). After getting the bucket index, you will use the remaining bits. Ranking is the term for determining the value that a bucket will have, though definitions are slightly different for different data structures.

One common ranking method is to find the position of the first 1 bit starting left to right using the remaining bits. If unable to find a 1, return the total number of bits then. Once the value and bucket is determined, pick the maximum between the value at the current bucket with the new ranking value.

There are variations on the ranking method so testing a lot is needed to ensure quality results.

This ranking is important because it will serve as the counter which the buckets store. The ranking will be used in calculating the cardinality.

Cardinality

Once you have enough information, the general formula to calculate the cardinality using LogLog is:

> **Cardinality = gamma function value x number of buckets x 2 ^ averageCount**

Average count is calculated by summing up all the values in the bucket then diving by the number of buckets.

Gamma function is a little complex, so I have given you a sufficient gamma value instead.

Take note, cardinality is not exact but rather an estimation.

Code

```java
import java.util.Arrays;
import java.util.Collection;

public class LogLog<T> {
    public interface Hasher<T> {
        long hash(T obj);
    }

    private int[] counter;
    private Hasher<T> hasher;
    private int neededBucketBits;
    private static final double GAMMA_VALUE =
0.39701;

    public LogLog(Hasher<T> hasher, int
numberOfCounters) {
        this.hasher = hasher;
        counter = new int[numberOfCounters];
        neededBucketBits =
Integer.toString(numberOfCounters, 2).length();
    }

    public void add(Collection<T> dataset) {
        for (T data : dataset) {
            String binaryForm =
getBinaryForm(hasher.hash(data));
            int bucketIndex =
Integer.parseInt(binaryForm.substring(0,
neededBucketBits), 2) % counter.length;
            int rank =
rank(binaryForm.substring(neededBucketBits));
```

```java
                        counter[bucketIndex] =
Math.max(counter[bucketIndex], rank);
            }
        }

        private static int rank(String binaryStr) {
                int rank =
findLeftmostOneBit(binaryStr);
                return rank != -1 ? rank :
binaryStr.length();
        }

        private static String getBinaryForm(long
hashcode) {
                return
addPadding(Long.toString(hashcode, 2));
        }

        private static String addPadding(String
binaryRepresentation) {
                return "0".repeat(64 -
binaryRepresentation.length()) + binaryRepresentation;
        }

        private static int findLeftmostOneBit(String
binaryStr) {
                return binaryStr.indexOf('1');
        }

        private double averageCount() {
                int sum = 0;
                for (int count : counter) {
                        sum += count;
                }
                return sum / (double) counter.length;
        }

        public double cardinality() {
                return GAMMA_VALUE * counter.length *
Math.pow(2, averageCount());
```

```
        }
}
```

Here is the full code. Most of it is rather straight forward.

This application does require you to create a hash function which as suggested before, try to implement the Murmur3 Hash function as it has resulted in good performance for this data structure.

Applications

Useful for whenever you need to find a quick estimate of unique things such as:

- IP Addresses
- DNA Sequences
- Devices hitting

Extension of LogLog

There is an improvement to LogLog which is known as **HyperLogLog**.

The main idea is the same however calculating the cardinality but has been proven to net better results.

Nonetheless, it is still important to understand the idea of how this came about and how you could modify this idea to fit your needs.

It takes a lot of playing around with and testing such as ranking algorithms, hash functions and buckets to ensure better results for your application.

Bloom Filter

Bloom Filter is a Probabilistic Data Structure that is used to determine whether **an element is present in a given list** of elements.

Bloom Filter is quite fast in element searching, however being probabilistic in nature it actually searches for an element being "**possibly in set**" or "**not in set at all**" which makes a crucial difference here and this is what makes Bloom Filter efficient and rapid in its approach.

The Bloom Filter Data Structure is closely associated with the Hashing Operation which plays an important role in this probabilistic data structure which we will further discuss. The advantages of this Data Structure is that it is Space Efficient and lightning fast while the disadvantages are that it is probabilistic in nature.

Even though Bloom Filters are quite efficient, the primary downside is its probabilistic nature. This can be understood with a simple example. Whenever a new element has to be searched in a List, there are chances that it might not be entirely in the list while similar chances are there that it might be in the set. If there is the possibility of the element in the set, then it could be a **false positive** or **true positive**.

If the element is not entirely present in the set, then it can be remarked as **true negative**. Due to its probabilistic nature, Bloom Filter can generate some false positive results also which means that the element is deemed to be present but it is actually not present. The point to be marked here is that a Bloom Filter never marks a false negative result which means it never signifies that an element is not present while it is actually present.

Understanding the Concept of Hashing and Bloom Filter

To understand the concept of Bloom Filter, we must first understand the concept of Hashing. Hashing is a computational process where a function is implemented which takes an input variable and it will return a distinct identifier for the element (usually an integer and within a given range). What makes Hashing so popular is that it is quite simple to implement and it is much more efficient compared to the conventional algorithms for performing various operations such as insertion and search.

In the Bloom Filter Data Structure, Hashing is an important concept. However, a Bloom Filter which holds a fixed number of elements can represent the set with many elements. While the numbers are added to the Bloom Filter Data Structure, the **false positive rate steadily increases** which is significant since Bloom Filter is a probabilistic data structure.

Unlike other Data Structures, **Deletion Operations is not possible** in the Bloom Filter because if we delete one element, we might end up deleting some other elements also, since hashing is used to clear the bits at the indexes where the elements are stored.

When a Bloom Filter is initialized, it is set as a Bit Array where all the elements are initialized to a default value. To insert an element, an integer value is needed which is hashed using a given Hash Function a given number of times. The bits are set into the Bit Vector and the indexes where the elements are added are initialized to 1.

The Search Operation in a Bloom Filter is also performed in the same manner.

Whenever a Search Query is passed, the index bit is checked to verify if the element is present or not. In case, any one of the index bits is not present, it is presumed that the element is not present in the Bloom Filter Vector. However, if all the bits are 1, then it is made sure that the element is present. There is no such case where it is presumed that a false is returned if an element is present.

Insertion and Search Operation in Bloom Filter

To insert an element into the Bloom Filter, every element goes through k hash functions. We will first start with an empty bit array with all the indexes initialized to zero and 'k' hash functions. The hash functions need to be independent and an optimal amount is calculated depending on the number of items that are to be hashed and the length of the table available with us.

The values to be inserted are hashed by all k hash functions and the bit in the hashed position is set to 1 in each case. Let us take some examples:

Insert 479: x=479, k1=2, k2=4

$k1 = (13 - (x \% 13))\% 7$, $k2 = (3 + 5x) \% 7$, etc.

0	1	2	3	4	5	6	7
0	1	1	0	1	0	0	0

k1 == 2, so we change bit 2 to a 1
k2 == 4, so we would change bit
3 to a 1, but it is already a 1.

To check if an element is already present in the Bloom Filter, we must again hash the search query and check if the bits are present or not. Let us take an example:

To check if 129 is in the table, just hash again and check the bits.
k1=1, k2=4: probably in the table!

0	1	2	3	4	5	6	7
0	1	1	0	1	0	0	0

$$k1 = (13 - (x \% 13)) \% 7, k2 = (3 + 5x) \% 7, \text{etc.}$$

As we discussed above, Bloom Filter can generate some false positive results also which means that the element is deemed to be present but it is actually not present. To find out the probability of getting a false positive result in an array of k bits is: $1-(1/k)$.

The pseudocode for insertion of an element in the Bloom Filter is as follows:

```
function insert(element)
{
    hash1=hashfunction(element)% Size_Of_Array
    hash2=hashfunction2(element)%Size_Of_Array
    array[hash1]=1;
    array[hash2]=1;
}
```

The pseudocode for searching an element in the Bloom Filter is as follows:

```
function search(element)
{
    hash1=h1(element)%Size_Of_Array;
    hash2=h2(element)%Size_Of_Array;
    if(array[hash1]==0 or array[hash2]==0)
    {
        return false;
    }
    else
    {
        prob = (1.0 - ((1.0 -
1.0/Size_Of_Array)**(k*Query_Size))) ** k
    }
    return "True";
}
```

Implementation of Bloom Filter

The following implementation is in Python 3 Programming Language which is a General-Purpose Programming Language:

```
import hashlib

class BloomFilter:
    def __init__(self, m, k):
        self.m = m
        self.k = k
        self.data = [0]*m
```

```python
        self.n = 0
    def insert(self, element):
        if self.k == 1:
            hash1 = h1(element) % self.m
            self.data[hash1] = 1
        elif self.k == 2:
            hash1 = h1(element) % self.m
            hash2 = h2(element) % self.m
            self.data[hash1] = 1
            self.data[hash2] = 1
        self.n += 1
    def search(self, element):
        if self.k == 1:
            hash1 = h1(element) % self.m
            if self.data[hash1] == 0:
                return "Not in Bloom Filter"
        elif self.k == 2:
            hash1 = h1(element) % self.m
            hash2 = h2(element) % self.m
            if self.data[hash1] == 0 or
self.data[hash2] == 0:
                return "Not in Bloom Filter"
        prob = (1.0 - ((1.0 -
1.0/self.m)**(self.k*self.n))) ** self.k
        return "Might be in Bloom Filter with false
positive probability "+str(prob)

def h1(w):
    h = hashlib.md5(w)
    return hash(h.digest().encode('base64')[:6])%10

def h2(w):
    h = hashlib.sha256(w)
    return hash(h.digest().encode('base64')[:6])%10
```

Advantages of Bloom Filter

The Time Complexity associated with Bloom Filter Data Structure is O(k) during Insertion and Search Operation where k is the number of hash function that have been implemented.

The Space Complexity associated with Bloom Filter Data Structure is O(m) where m is the Size of the Array.

While a hash table uses only one hash function, Bloom Filter uses multiple Hash Functions to avoid collisions.

With this, you will have the complete knowledge of the working of Bloom Filter. We will, now, dive into the applications of Bloom Filter.

Applications of Bloom Filter

Bloom Filter is memory efficient than a Hash Map with the same performance. The only thing to note is that this is a probabilistic data structure so for a small number of cases, it may give wrong results (which can be limited).

The applications of Bloom Filter are:

- Weak password detection
- Internet Cache Protocol
- Safe browsing in Google Chrome
- Wallet synchronization in Bitcoin
- Hash based IP Traceback
- Cyber security like virus scanning

We will now understand each of the applications of Bloom Filter in depth.

Weak password detection

The idea is that the system can maintain a list of weak passwords in a form of Bloom Filter. This can be updated whenever a new user enters a password or an existing user updates the password.

Whenever, a new user comes, the new password is checked in the Bloom Filter and if a potential match is detected then the user is warned.

Note that passwords should be stored in hashed form to ensure that even if the Bloom Filter data becomes public, the password of the users are safe.

You can see this application as a string matching application which is memory efficient and works as fast as a Hash Map.

Internet Cache Protocol

A network system uses Proxies which are computer systems through which all network requests are sent and received. This provides a central point of contact within a computer network system.

A Proxy hashes all URLs and keep them in its own cache. As there are multiple proxies in the network, all proxies share their cache record with each other. This is known as Internet Cache Protocol.

Consider a case when a computer A wants to go to "iq.opengenus.org".

The GET request will go to its nearest proxy P1. Now, proxy P1 will check its cache record and may find out that this page (iq.opengenus.org) has been cached by proxy P3. So, proxy P1 will send a request to proxy P3 and get the page and will return it to the computer A. The searching in the cache is done using Bloom Filter as you can imagine that internet use history of multiple users will be large.

As Bloom Filter is a probabilistic data structure, it may give wrong prediction like:

Proxy P1 says URL is cached in P3 but it is not cached.

This will send a request to P3 but it will return that the page is not cached. Hence, the next request will be sent to ISP. This results in one extra request (P1 to P3).

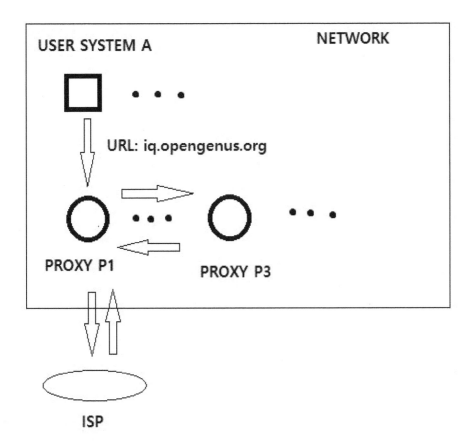

One problem is that proxies delete pages after some time, but Bloom Filter does not have an feature to delete entries from it. The solution is avoiding this extra traffic due clearing of proxy's cache is to use **Counting Bloom Filter**.

Safe browsing in Google Chrome

Google Chrome uses Bloom Filter to check if an URL is a threat or not. If Bloom Filter says that it is a threat, then it goes to another round of testing before alerting the user.

Wallet synchronization in Bitcoin

Bitcoin is using Bloom Filter due to its efficient performance and it minimizes the risk of triggering DDoS attacks.

In Bitcoin, all information of blocks are distributed between nodes and as this data is large, this makes the system slow down. The problem is most of the data is thrown away after being received. So, Bloom Filter is used to detect if a particular information will be deleted later or not and following it, the decision to transfer data is made.

Hash based IP Traceback

A challenge in designing IP protocols is to track the computer from which a packet has originated. This is difficult due to packet forwarding techniques such as NAT and encapsulation even in the case where there is no attempt to hide the source.

The solution is to use a Hash based approach to maintain audit traces which can be used to track the origin machine. As the amount of internet network is large, Bloom Filter is used for this.

Cyber security like virus scanning

Common applications of Bloom Filter in the field of Cyber Security are:

- Virus scanning
- Worm detection
- DDoS prevention
- Risky URL detection

The basic idea is to search sub-string (of the data at hand) of a specific size within a Bloom Filter for that specific size. The idea of using specific size is that searching can be done in parallel. If Bloom Filter predicts that there may be a match, then the sub-string is checked in a Hash Map to be sure.

The use of Bloom Filters in this makes the entire process quite fast and reliable at the same time.

With this, you must have a strong understanding of how Bloom Filters can be used in real life. Enjoy.

Skip List

A skip list is a **Probabilistic Data Structure** that is used for storing a sorted list of items with a help of multiple linked lists and is used to **search an element efficiently**.

A skip list allows the lookup process to be more efficient in terms of space and time complexity. The skip list data structure skips over many of the items of the full list in one step so "skip" is in the name.

In simple terms, skip list is a modified linked list which allows for fast search.

It consists of a base Linked List holding the elements, together with a tower of lists maintaining a linked hierarchy of subsequences, each skipping over fewer elements.

Description

A skip list is built in layers:

- The bottom layer is a linked list with all the sorted elements
- Each higher layer (linked list) acts as an "express lane" for the lists below, where an element in layer i appears in layer i+1 with some fixed probability p (p is usually 0.25).
- On average, each element appears in 1/(1-p) lists (=4/3) and the topmost element (usually a special head element at the front of the skip list) appears log1/pn lists.

A search for a target element begins at the head element in the top list and proceeds horizontally until the current element is greater than or equal to the target.

If the current element is equal to the target, it has been found.

If the current element is greater than the target, the procedure is repeated after returning to the previous element. By choosing different values of p, it is possible to trade search costs against storage costs.

P increases; Storage increases; Search time decreases;

Working

We create multiple layers of Linked Lists so that we can skip some nodes. See the following example list with 16 nodes and two layers (can be more layers):

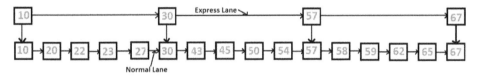

The upper layer has few nodes and connects to nodes in between of the lower linked list. This allows us to traverse the upper linked list and skip nodes of the lower linked list.

Suppose we want to search for 40.

We start from first node of upper linked list and keep moving till we find a node whose next element is greater than 40. Once we find such a node (30), we move to lower linked list using pointer from this node, and search for 40 using the same process. In following example, we start from 30 on the lower linked list and with linear search, we find 40.

Why is this probabilistic?

This data structure is probabilistic as we are skipping elements based on a probability factor and hence, it is similar to a Binary Tree with the exception that balancing is not strict.

This data structure will always result in the correct answer and the only probabilistic nature is in the structure and distribution of elements across different levels.

Basic Operations

Following are the operations performed on Skip list:

- Insertion Operation: To Insert any element in a list
- Search Operation: To Search any element in a list
- Deletion Operation: To Delete any element from a list

Insertion Operation

To insert a new element, we need to determine in which level (linked list) the element will be inserted. The level is determined by a random algorithm depending on the set probability p.

Level does not depend on the number of elements in the node. The level for node is decided by the following algorithm:

```
randomLevel()
      level = 1
      //random() that returns a random value in
[0...1)
      while random() < p and level < MaxLevel:
```

```
        level = level + 1
    return level
```

MaxLevel is the upper bound on number of levels in the skip list.

It can be determined as **MaxLevel = log (p/2(N))**.

Above algorithm assure that random level will never be greater than MaxLevel. Here p is the fraction of the nodes with level i pointers also having level i+1 pointers and N is the number of nodes in the list.

Node Structure

Each node has:

- a key
- a forward array for pointers to nodes of a different level
- A level i node carries i forward pointers indexed through 0 to i.

Node

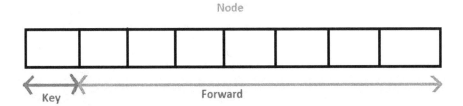

Key   Forward

We will start from highest level in the list and compare key of next node of the current node with the key to be inserted. Basic idea is:

- Key of next node is less than key to be inserted then we keep on moving forward on the same level

---

- Key of next node is greater than the key to be inserted then we store the pointer to current node i at update[i] and move one level down and continue our search.

Pseudocode for Insertion

```
Insert(list, searchKey)
define update[0...MaxLevel+1]
x = list.header // top most element
for i from list->level to 0:
        while x.forward[i].key < forward[i].key
                update[i] = x
                x = x->forward[0]


lvl = randomLevel()
if lvl > list->level:
        for i from list->level + 1 to lvl do
                update[i] = list->header
                list->level = lvl


x = makeNode(lvl, searchKey, value)
for i from 0 to level:
        x->forward[i] = update[i]->forward[i]
update[i]->forward[i] = x
```

Here update[i] holds the pointer to node at level i from which we moved down to level i-1 and pointer of node left to insertion position at level 0.

Example

Starting with an empty Skip list with MAXLEVEL 4, Suppose we want to insert these following keys with their "Randomly Generated Levels":

5 with level 1, 26 with level 1, 25 with level 4, 6 with level 3, 21 with level 1, 3 with level 2, 22 with level 2 .

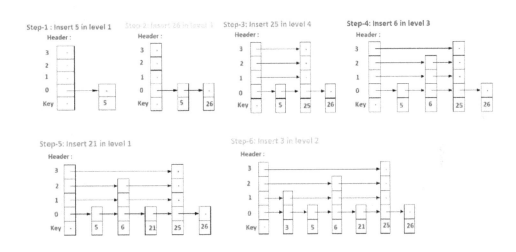

Now, at Step-7 where we need to insert 22 in level 2 we need to go through some following details:

The insert algorithm maintains two local variables (besides the skip list header):

- X, a pointer which points to a node whose forward pointers point to nodes whose key we are currently comparing to the key we want to insert this lets us quickly compare keys, and follow forward pointers.
- update, an array of node pointers which point to nodes whose forward pointers may need to be updated to point to the newly inserted node, if the new node is inserted in the list just before the node X points to this lets us quickly update all the pointers necessary to splice in the new node

---

Inserting 22 in level 2: frame 1

Follow top-level pointer: 25 > 22, so drop down and follow pointer: 6 < 22, so update

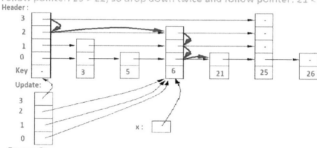

Frame 2:

Follow pointer: 25 > 22, so drop down twice and follow pointer: 21 < 22, so update

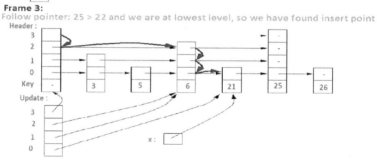

Frame 3:

Follow pointer: 25 > 22 and we are at lowest level, so we have found insert point

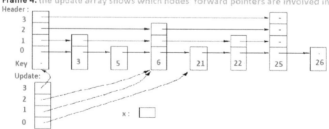

Frame 4: the update array shows which nodes' forward pointers are involved in the insert

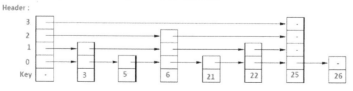

Here is the skip list after all keys have been inserted :

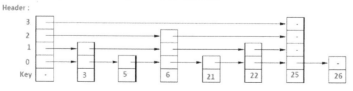

© OpenGenus [Probabilistic Data Structures]

Searching Operation

Searching an element is very similar to approach for searching a spot for inserting an element in Skip list. The basic idea is if:

1. Key of next node is less than search key then we keep on moving forward on the same level.

2. Key of next node is greater than the key to be inserted then we store the pointer to current node i at update[i] and move one level down and continue our search.

At the lowest level (0), if the element next to the rightmost element (update[0]) has key equal to the search key, then we have found key otherwise failure.

Pseudocode for Searching:

```
Search(list, searchKey)
        x = list->header
        for key < level to 0 do
                while x->forward[i]->key < forward[i].key
                        x = x->forward[0]
        if x -> key = searchKey
                then return x->value
        else return failure
```

Example of Searching

Consider this example where we want to search for key 17:

Now to search for key in a skip list we will follow the steps of our Pseudocode.

Here, the idea is that we will compare the key values of every node with our search key (ie 17). if the key of next node is greater than our key 17 then we keep on moving on that same level otherwise we store the pointer to current node i at update[i] and move one level down and continue our search. Here, we will stop at which the key of next node is 19 (ie 17 < 19) and store pointer of that node.

Deletion Operation

Deletion of an element K is done as follows:

- Locate element K in the Skip list
- Rearrangement of pointers is done to remove element from list just like we do in singly linked list.
- We start from lowest level and do rearrangement until element next to update[i] is not K. After deletion of element K, there could be levels with no elements, so we will remove these empty levels and decrement the level of Skip list.

Pseudocode for Deletion

```
Delete(list, searchKey)
update[0 … MaxLevel+1]

x = list->header
for i from list->level to 0:
    while x->forward[i]->key < forward[i]
        update[i] = x
x = x->forward[0]
if x->key = searchKey then
    for i from 0 to list->level
        if update[i]->forward[i] != x then
```

```
            break
        update[i]->forward[i] = x->forward[i]
    free(x)
// Remove empty levels
while list->level > 0 and list->header->forward[list-
>level] = NIL
    list->level = list->level - 1
```

Example of deletion

Consider this example where we want to delete element 6.

Deletion of an element 6 is preceded by locating this element 6 in the
Skip list using above mentioned search algorithm. Once 6 is located,
rearrangement of pointers is done to remove 6 from list just like we do in
singly linked list.

First, we must find the preceding node that is 3 and identify the nodes
whose pointers may need to be reset. Next, we must reset the pointers
to the targeted node "around" it (that is 7), and finally we deallocate the
targeted node (3).

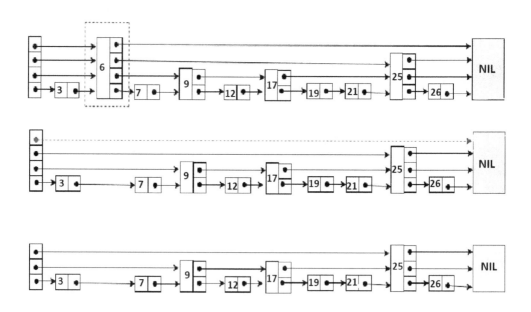

Here at level 3, there is no element (arrow in red) after deleting element 6. So we will decrement level of skip list by 1.

Complexity

Time Complexity:

Operation	Average Case	Worst Case
Search	O(log N)	O(N)
Insert	O(log N)	O(N)
Delete	O(log N)	O(N)

Space Complexity: O(N log N)

The Search, insert, and delete operations on ordinary binary search trees are efficient, O(log n), when the input data is random; but less efficient, O(n), when the input data are ordered. Skip List performance for these same operations and for any data set is about as good as that of randomly-built binary search trees that is O(log N).

In an ordinary sorted linked list, Search, insert, and delete are in O(n) because the list must be scanned node-by-node from the head to find the relevant node. If we could scan down the list in bigger steps (skip down, as it were), we would reduce the cost of scanning. This is the fundamental idea behind Skip Lists.

We speak of a Skip List node having levels, one level per forward reference. The number of levels in a node is called the size of the node.

In an ordinary sorted list, insert, delete, and search operations require sequential traversal of the list. This results in O(n) performance per operation. Skip Lists allow intermediate nodes in the list to be skipped during a traversal - resulting in an expected performance of O(log n) per operation.

Advantages

- Skip lists perform very well in practice compared to BST and Hash Tables
- We can get the next element in constant time (Same operation takes logarithmic time for inorder traversal for BST and linear time in hash tables).
- Can be modified to more wider applications like segment tree + skip list, indexable skip lists, or keyed priority queue.
- It does well in persistent (slow) storage

Disadvantages

- skip lists take more space than BST
- skip lists are not cache friendly

Significance in Real Life/ Conclusion

Probabilistic Data Structures are used in real life more widely as expected. This is mainly attributed to its advantages (mainly, low memory) and error resistant systems.

Let us summarize the Probabilistic Data Structures we studied quickly:

- Count Min Sketch: Keeps track of frequency of each element (alternative to Hash Map)
- MinHash: Finds similarity between two sets
- LogLog: Finds number of unique elements in a set
- Bloom Filter: Finds element in a set (Alternative to Hash Map)
- Skip List: Finds element in a set (alternative to Linked List)

Consider the example of Bloom Filter.

Chrome browser maintains a cache of several resources and also, a list of cached resources. This list is large as one visit several web resources.

The most obvious approach to check if it is cached is to convert the list into a hash map and use it for searching. This is not preferred as a hash map consumes significant memory which can be used to store resources. Moreover, browser has limited memory available for use.

For this, Chrome uses Bloom Filter which uses significantly less memory than Hash Map and delivers performance same as Hash Map.

In the worst case, the answer returned by Bloom Filter is wrong and we end up checking the cache records and not find the resource. In this case, Chrome sends a request to fetch the resource. The slight overhead in this case plays out in good performance overall.

Similar is the case with other Probabilistic Data Structures.

Skip List is a notable example and should be used in place of Linked List if slightly more memory is available for use. This is unique as the answer returned by Skip List is always correct and it can be used as a Linked List as well in the worst case.

Consider a Probabilistic Data Structure in your next work and see if it brings in some advantage.

Learn Computing for FREE at **iq.OpenGenus.org** and get occasional FREE gifts and books.

iq.opengenus.org

discuss.opengenus.org

team@opengenus.org

amazon.opengenus.org

linkedIn.opengenus.org

github.opengenus.org

twitter.opengenus.org

facebook.opengenus.org

instagram.opengenus.org

Events in life are not certain so are in Data Structures.

Enjoy this new knowledge.